August '11

Peek-a-Boo, Baby

Luana K. Mitten

ROURKE PUBLISHING
www.rourkepublishing.com

www.rourkepublishing.com

PHOTO CREDITS: Title Page: © Diana McKinney; Page 3: © ArtisticCaptures; Page 4: © Twildlife; Page 5: © Szefei; Page 6: © Cardiae Page 7: © Leah-Anne Thompson; Page 8: © doubtfulneddy; Page 9: © iofoto; Page 10: © Pakhnyushchyy; Page 11: © Anatols; Page 12: © Katerinasamsonova; Page 13: © Jennifer Russel; Page 14: © Billysiew; Page 15: © James Martin; Page 16: © Gelpi; Page 17: © GOH SIOK HIAN; Page 18: © Photobunnyuk; Page 19: © Darren Baker; Page 20, 21: © Cathy Yeulet; Page 22: © Gelpi; © Cardiae, © Twildlife, © Photobunnyuk; Page 23: © Katerinasamsonova, © Billysiew, © doubtfulneddy, © © Pakhnyushchyy; Illustrations: © TZU-LAN HSIEH

Editor: Meg Greve

Cover design by Nicola Stratford, Blue Door Publishing

Page design by Renee Brady

Library of Congress Cataloging-in-Publication Data

Mitten, Luana K.
  Peek-a-boo, baby / Luana K. Mitten.
     p. cm. -- (Animal babies and me)
  Includes bibliographical references and index.
  ISBN 978-1-61590-262-0 (Hard Cover) (alk. paper)
  ISBN 978-1-61590-502-7 (Soft Cover)
  1. Animals--Infancy--Juvenile literature. 2. Guessing games--Juvenile literature. I. Title.
  QL763.M58 2011
  591.3'9--dc22
                                                   2010010107

Rourke Publishing
Printed in the United States of America, North Mankato, Minnesota
033010
033010LP

www.rourkepublishing.com - rourke@rourkepublishing.com
Post Office Box 643328 Vero Beach, Florida 32964

Peek-a-boo,

I spy a **kangaroo**.

Peek-a-scamper,

I spy a **hamster**.

Peek-a-bounce,

I spy a **puppy**.

Peek-a-squirm,

I spy a **worm**.

Peek-a-prance,

I spy a **pony**.

Peek-a-swing,

I spy a **monkey**.

Peek-a-swish,

I spy a **fish**.

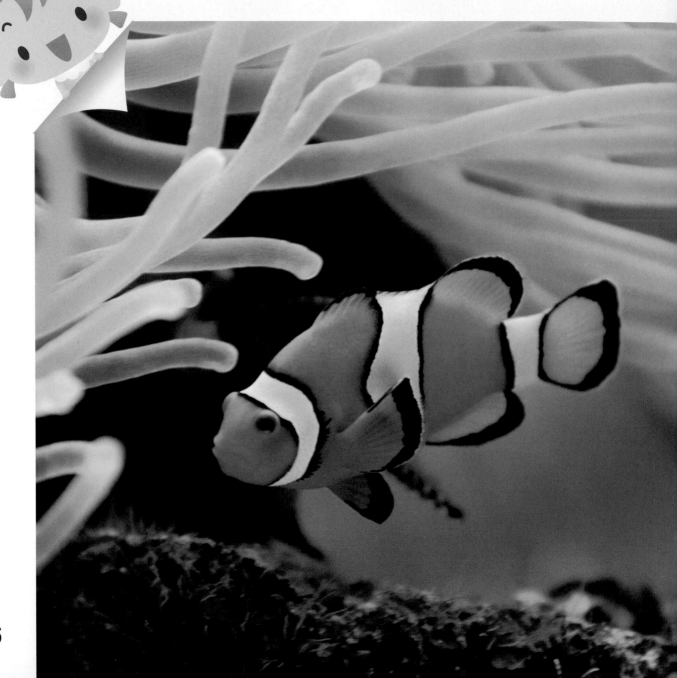

Peek-a-pounce,

I spy a **kitten**.

Peek-a-squeeze,

I spy huggable you!

Picture Glossary

fish (FISH): An animal with scales, fins, and gills. Fish live in rivers, lakes, and oceans.

hamster (HAM-stur): A small, furry animal that is often kept as a pet in a cage.

kangaroo (kang-guh-ROO): An animal with short front legs and long back legs. A mother kangaroo carries her baby in a pouch on her stomach.

kitten (KIT-uhn): A kitten is a young cat. It takes about a week after a kitten is born for its eyes and ears to open.

monkey (MUHNG-kee): An animal with hands and feet that are used for climbing and holding.

pony (POH-nee): An animal that looks like a small horse, but stays small even when it is full grown.

puppy (PUHP-ee): A puppy is a young dog. Puppies are born without teeth.

worm (WURM): An animal that has a long, soft body with no arms or legs.

Index

Websites

www.kids.nationalgeographic.com/Animals

www.timeforkids.com/TFK/kids/games

www.enchantedlearning.com/subjects/animals/Animalbabies.shtml

About the Author

Luana Mitten lives in Tampa, Florida and does not like the way snakes play peek-a-boo with her when she is digging in her garden. Luana wishes the snakes would peek-a-shoo!